TEMPLES OF SAND

TEMPLES OF SAND

By
DMRSekhar

KALPAZ

ISBN : 978-81-783-5914-4

First Published, 2018

Published by

Kalpaz Publications
C-30, Satyawati Nagar,
Delhi – 110052
Ph.: 011-47034999, 9811692060
www.kalpazpublications.com
E-mail: kalpaz@hotmail.com

Printed at: G. Print Process, Delhi

Dedication

I dedicate, Temples of Sand, the collection of my English poems to Sri. P.K. Deb IAS, who reposed so much confidence in me as Managing Director of M/s Rajasthan State Mines and Minerals Ltd. by giving me challenging jobs. I hope I did not disappoint him.

Contents

Foreword by Tomichan Matheikal 11
Prologue 15

Conflict 17
An old dream 18
Mahan 19
Desert dancer 20
God is insufficient 21
Bronze and gold 22
Salt and camphor 23
Horned rabbit 24
Prime 25
Cold wings 26
The winners 27
Alive! 28
Tandavam 29
Raging fire 30
I think of you 31
Award 32
Still in love 33
Mother 34
In the jungle 35
The show 36
Dog of a time 37
Mr. Right 38
A heart slit apart 39

Bee 40
Tsunami 41
Repair 42
Left and right 43
Philosophical cat 44
Knell 45
Nude 46
Peace 47
Skull dance 48
A world of love 49
Bleeding 50
Debate 51
Collapse of the universe 52
Half moon 53
Was that you? 54
Return of a kiss 55
Elite 56
That and this 57
Warmonger 58
Nobble 59
Dear crows 60
The wisest 61
Lost child 62
Nest 63
That is love 64
Key 65
Portrait of love 66
Strangers 67
Sophistry 68
Being big 69
O chandamama 70
Entangled 71
Her mind 72
Poetlet 73
Child 74

Dog 75
Promise 76
Mad 77
Young Varun 78
Lost 79
Thomas Doubting 80
Night queen 81
Queen 82
Let us fly 83
Gush and glair 84
Animal farm 85
Day time moon 86
Escape 87
Soliloquy 88
Lap top 89
Do not quit 90
Hope 91
Hamsafar 92
Prayer of a Beggar 93
A request 94
Refugee 95
Restless vulture 96
Lonely I await 97
That night when you came 98
Bubbles 99
Fly's dialogue 100
Tell me why 101
Dead sea 102
Sun, you and me 103
Boundary conditions 104
As I don't know 105
Oh you 106
Temples of sand 107
If love exists 108
Companion 109

Chakravaka 110
Wine 111
Sivaranjani 112
To be with her 113
The tigress 114
You and me 115
Wise and the foolish alike 116
Life 117
Sweet Nothings 118
Ye 119
New creation 120
Kavita 121
The suspect 122
Fate of a poem 123
Burma 124
Man in Hell 125
A man in stone 126
Traitor 127
Native 128
On a rainy morning 129
At Home 130
The road to nowhere 131
Oh my fish 132
A rose in solitude 133
Setting sun 134
A girl in prayer 135

Foreword

And the factory is humming at full production
Just over the hill, making money,
Whispering, a big fish without eyes,
The most profound unhappiness.

Emblems, Douglas Dunn

The world has become so prosaic today that poetry has almost vanished from its literature. If poetry still survives, it does so in some unexpected and rather pragmatic domains such as architecture and horticulture. There are some buildings, flyover conglomerates or parks which embody the human quest for the poetic. They are rare too. Utilitarianism has become such a dominant guiding principle in every sphere of human activity today that there is little place left for beauty to find expression. Poetry cannot be born without some yearning for the beautiful.

When science started dominating the human civilisation, beauty took a backseat. Science brought new and newer technologies which made life better and more comfortable for the human species. When the German philosopher, Hegel, said that the rhythm of poetry serves to lift us into a world quite different from that of prose or everyday life, he was obliquely referring to the beauty that is inevitably embodied in poetry.

The European movement known as Enlightenment was a genuine attempt to release mankind from the dark forces in the mind which led people to superstitions and subhuman activities. Enlightenment focused on the noble human quality of reason. Eventually science and technology reaped rich harvests by putting human rational faculty to good use. Today, in the first quarter of the 21st century, we stand inundated with technology. Many of the blessings of that technology are also a curse.

Dealing with redundancy is perhaps the biggest curse. A product like a mobile phone or a car or a computer becomes outdated even before we have learnt to use all of its features. The product is replaced with a newer version. Too many old versions become redundant too soon. The redundancy has affected human relationships too. Utilitarianism has almost become the sole criterion of relationships.

Science cannot be blamed for this sad situation. Socio-economic policies are not made by science. The neo-liberal policies that drive the global affairs today evolved out of a complex network of forces. Competition and acquisition have become the major driving forces of today's global system. Both these– competitiveness and acquisitiveness – are essentially isolating forces. They isolate one man from another. They motivate each person to see the other as either a rival to be defeated or a tool to be used for one's own benefit.

While science and technology offered a more comfortable, or at least a less laborious, life, neo-liberalism held out the promise of an affluent life with increased wealth-creation. Both comfort and wealth are positive factors. Yet, after three centuries of technological revolution and three decades of economic revolution, the world has not become any better place than earlier for most people. On the contrary, some beautiful things like poetry nearly vanished from the world. The decampment of poetry is just a symptom of a deeper malaise that is afflicting the human civilisation today.

The real malaise that has gripped civilisation today is man's alienation from the deeper cores of his being. Erich Fromm distinguished between two basic orientations toward life: having and being. A having orientation reflects a person's competitive concern with possessing and consuming resources. This orientation is fostered by technological societies, he argued. The being mode, in contrast, focuses on what one *is*. It focuses on sharing rather than competition.

Today's world does not encourage the being mode. When we are constantly competing to *appear* better than the other, we cannot be our real selves. We are forced to put on masks. Masks do not have feelings and emotions except those which are painted on them. Masks cannot have poetry in their being.

We have reached the "profound unhappiness" of masks.

Travelling inward, into the deepest cores of our hearts, is the solution. Being in deeper touch with our emotions and the poetry that is throbbing in those emotions is one remedy to the ills that plague contemporary civilisation.

Some of the most profound truths lie in poetry.

Reason and science deal with the material world, with things as they are in themselves. To that extent, they bring us 'objective' truths. But man does not live by objective truths alone. In fact, quite many of his truths are subjective.

Human beings are concerned not only with understanding things as they are in themselves, but also with the impact of those things on their emotions. On the one hand, as W H Hudson said, "When science has provided us with its completest rationale of things, we are still primarily impressed by their mystery and beauty." On the other hand, there are many recesses in the human mind which are not satisfied by purely rational answers. Otherwise, evil would not have found a place in the human world.

"Poetry begins where matter of fact or of science ceases to be merely such, and to exhibit a further truth..." said Leigh Hunt. While truth in science is fidelity to facts, in poetry it is "fidelity to our emotional apprehension of facts, to the impression which they make upon us, to the feelings of pleasure or pain, hope or fear, wonder or religious reverence, which they arouse" (W H Hudson).

That is why poetry is more relevant today than ever. We need poetry to take us back to our heart and its profound yearnings.

D M R Sekhar's present collection, *Temples of Sand*, consists of poems that aspire to take us back to our hearts. Most of the poems in this collection are brief and to the point. They do not seek to make a point, however. Like all good poems, they seize the reader's imagination and work on it slowly. They let the reader's imagination do the rest of the work. Poems like 'Sun, you and me,' 'Mad' and the title poem 'Temples of Sand' are just a few examples. Most of the poems contain the fundamental truths of life which a poet brings to the reader through the unique prism of his imagination. For example, 'Raging Fire,' or 'Alive'. Arresting metaphors are the greatest wealth in a poem. Poems like 'An old dream,' 'The Tigress' and 'Night Queen' reveal the poet's exquisite skill in producing such metaphors.

While there is much Romantic longing in many of the poems, many contemporary evils are dealt with much sensitivity. Occasionally the whole history from Kurukshetra to the Vietnam War gets telescoped in a few lines ('Skull dance'), or the poet merges into the cosmic dance riding the wave of just six lines (*Tandavam*). A few of the poems are marked by remarkable wit and drama too: 'Mr Right' and 'The Wisest,' for example. There are many poems in which the poet implies the insignificance of his own being as a poet.

Most of the poems eloquently, though subtly sometimes, bring out the essential ironies and paradoxes of life, which scientific truths and economic approaches will not be able to perceive. That is why these poems will strike a chord in the reader's heart.

Tomichan Matheikal

Prologue

Reading and enjoying poetry is one thing and writing poems is another which is entirely a different cup of tea. During 1979 I wrote cadila cross inspired by a picture of a girl in prayer in the calendar of Cadila company. After that I could not write a single poem. 1979 was a period of troubled transition for me. From super active students politics of Andhra University I came to Zawar Mines to work as a mineral process engineer for M/s Hindustan Zinc ltd.(HZL). It was quiet unexpected for we were selected by HZL during an in campus interview that is without formally applying for a job. Before that I was a Ph.D scholar in the department of Chemical Engineering, Andhra University. Living in North India without knowing Hindi is in itself another problem. Out side the mineral processing plant at Zawar life was about aloofness. Hence I used to spend as many hours as possible in the plant even out side of eight duty hours. Indeed that helpless aloofness forced me to express my self in the form of "cadila cross". Then we quickly picked up the language and also the tricks of running a mineral processing plant. Since then mineral processing is not only a profession to me but also became a passion particularly research in sulfide mineral processing. The words Sphalerite, Galena and Xanthate became stimulants to me so much so that my daughter was later named as Xanthate!

My success in handling Phosphate Beneficiation plant at Jhamarkotra brought me to Eshidiya Phosphate Beneficiation Plant, which was running at a low capacity since 1995 to 2006.

I came to Jordan with my team of engineers during the year 2007 and we did put Eshidiya Plant on the tracks. Eshidiya is in the middle of Sahara desert and we find nothing there except the mining and beneficiation activities. Away from the children and Indu it is aloofness again. Our success at Eshidiya Plant made me popular among the operators of Phosphate Beneficiation Plants in different countries. But personal life has become Zero. Aloofness is maddening. Then I logged into the Social Network http://www.sulekha.com/ where blogging is freedom. I started posting blogs on topics of my interest including some poems. Raj Arumugam, D. Sampat and Matheikal, T encouraged my poems and I tried more without bothering too much on the use of English language. The Present collection "Temples of Sand" are the poems I wrote since last four years plus the one I wrote during 1979. I wish and intend to gift this collection in printed version to my friends instead of putting to commercial purpose. Thanks to Sri Amit Garg, for immediately accepting to publish this collection on my behalf when I met him at Delhi in his office. Hope my readers will enjoy my poems.

DM Rathna Sekhar

Conflict

Weeping inconsolably, that was my heart
I can't stop but laugh at it
Me and my heart always in conflict!

An old dream

While searching for something else
I saw this old dream, torn and dilapidated
Hazy letters were trying to remind some thing
Taken aback I slipped it back into my heart

Mahan

Dhan chahat nish din adham
Madhyam chahat dhan aur maan
Uttam chahat maan hie
Kachoo na chahe mahaan.

Which may translate to

Mahan

The mean desire money, day and night
The middle desire money, sans a slight
The genuine desire only and only the status
Desires the Mahan neither money nor kudos

Who is the author of that Hindi poem?

Desert dancer

No not a deserted heart
It is the heart of the desert
Look at the dunes of sand
Listen the tunes of the band

Let's dance with them
With wilderness to the brim

God is insufficient

Easy is to teach, a man ignorant
Pleasant it is to teach a brilliant
For an idiot who is non prudent
Even God is, grossly insufficient

A poem by Bhartru Hari.
Not a true translation.

Bronze and gold

The simpleton speaks always aloud
Gentle men are cool and never proud
The bronze barks and makes a drama
Gold's voice no noise, listen ye Vema

A poem of Yogi Vemana.
Not a true translation.

Salt and camphor

Camphor and salt look very much alike
When tasted, the difference will speak
Different are the people with stamina
Quality comes first, listen ye Vemana

A poem by Vemana a Telugu poet.
Not true translation.

Horned rabbit

Oil from sands ye may squeeze
Water from mirage still at ease
Ye may find a horned rabbit
Never try to convince an idiot

A Bhartru Hari poem.
Not a true translation to its Telugu version.

Prime

Wasted, yes, a life time how?
Really for whom, I do not know!
In my heart lives that rhyme,
Unsung but, she still is prime!

Cold wings

Dreams yes, those unviable transient things
Haunt me in my dreams, with cold wings
That can't fly me any where
But I love them, I swear

The winners

We were thrown out and displaced
Yet we were not very much displeased
Were insulted and were tried
But we never felt tired
In us nothing could instill fears
For this land is originally ours, only ours

Alive!

We are alive, not as we willed
With certain death, life is filled
Why keep then, ourselves grilled?
Hey my friend let us get thrilled

Tandavam

the Sun is gone
stars awaiting the Moon
on the top i stand alone
and hear the wind's moan
the stars say, Sekhar come
let us sing, dance and drum

30-3-2008

Raging fire

the truth will spread out
even if ye hide it
as if a raging fire
await a nightmare ye, liar

I think of you

then, the moon appears as if a big star
and the sun as one put in a small jar
I think of the past and of you dear
memories come alive, the past is near
nothing to ask, no explanations to offer
I just observe, sans feelings, none to suffer
the drama of life, a flashback, runs fast
that is when, in a cup of wine, I get lost

Award

with flowers ye decorate my tomb
for dreams that died in the womb
in love I was and am, for no reward
why tears now? posthumous award?

Still in love

look, do not weep, tears I hate
tear off that thing they call fate
once upon a time and even now
strangers we are, still in love

Mother

then it was that Mush
now it is this Bush
they destroy my peace
Mother Earth I am, please.

In the jungle

far away from the idiotic mob
there you my tigress my cub
in the wild lap of the nature
care free, fearless of future
for none, you are keen
yet ye still the queen

The show

my mind today stands still
as if emptied sans any will
who I am and where will I go
unknown yet goes on the show

Dog of a time

please come, come on new year
I believe not thee though dear
yet ye came all thy excuses lame
ye shy why ye no new dame

ask me not how much in shame
you put me last time you came
riots murders wail of women
come clean this time please listen

Mr. Right

Yes Sir, I am always right;
and not only that -
some how
you are always wrong!
I am right
even
when I do not know
what you are talking about -
as you are wrong
even before opening the topic!

A heart slit apart

can you see the pain in my heart
the weal failing to heal as it slit apart
upon the corpse ye ate the rotten feast
worst ye, stinking ugly nasty beast

12-12-2007

Note:

The stomach of a pregnant woman was slit opened and the foetus was removed only to char it with its mother. The only sin of the woman is that she was a Muslim by birth and so inadvertently. There are worst people than the murderer, those who approve of the murder most foul. I ask, had it been your mother when you were in her womb? Your wife when she was bearing your child? In case if it is your daughter the one you so loved? Those who approve of that act are elite of this country! Above all patriots? Saviors of my Mother Land?

Mera Bharat Mahan?

Let us say sorry for what had happened both in Godhra / Ahmadabad and also for what is happening in W. Bengal.

Bee

my silence
not thy license
come to sense
or else
I shall lance

11-12-2007

Tsunami

ye sure vanquished me
I returned as tsunami
take that long to build
I shall blast ye behold

20-12-2007

Repair

an old unsold rancid wine
stinking stuff worth only to drain
in a bottle new ye fill fine
cheating? how long? now refrain
why waging a losing battle in vain?
come on I shall repair thy brain!

10-12-2007.

Left and right

present society has an error
they plead and spread all terror
a theory, a religion they do refer
do not mind if people suffer

you are right when you left
right is rogue if causing rift
left and right both are wrong
middle path is always strong

10-12-2007.

Philosophical cat

The cat that caught
a philosophical thought!
it has to do what?
with poem or the poet?
perhaps naught!

may be of a rat
that got long lost
or became a ghost
a thought being wrought
an idea being brought
for excuse to be sought

why ye shout
is it not my right?
to survive? to eat?

8-12-2007

Knell

different stories ye all tell
and command me not to yell
usurped the lands I dwell
well, I shall ring thy death knell

3-12-2007

Nude

set me free and let me go
far far away onto the rainbow
leaving to sway all that nurture
love with wine to live in nature

30-11-2007

Peace

from me you are never away
flip flopping as a moon's ray
you, in my mind I always find
can't miss despite daily grind
ye frozen to silence in time's wrap
yet sonorous, behind a misty drape

I know, this run futile a row
of what use then, all this show
not knowing what to fulfill
we run until, into the standstill

dream, of having spreading wings
sans the slings, out of trappings
to fly and reach eternal grace
with Thee to stay only in peace

25-11-2007

Skull dance

Origin

crawling this evening, my mind so dull
before me dancing, many a skull
few are new, some old, others ancient
some have glorious stories to lament
arrived after huge blood spills
some are the killers and other the kills
from the fields of history, a mayhem
a jolt, a revolt, kuruskhetra, or Vietnam

Helpless

how many came? prophet after prophet
none could stop, this game of profit
end of the game
human remained the game

Dance

foul smells dancing skulls
unknown spells evil skills
crawling here crawling there
sprawling sprawling every where

22.11.2007

A world of love

is there a world bereft of tears
without wars and without fears
there are only flowers and lovers
where human dignity never lowers
a leaderless society sans poverty
sans priority, majority or minority
that world I shall bring to earth
and ensure that love not in dearth

23-11-2007

Bleeding

reasons different, killings same
dead are human, excuses lame
Gujara, Banga all in shame
Nation bleeding, whom to blame?
both say, they are correct
babu, tell me can you resurrect?

22-11-2007

Debate

Oh learned wise ye fine excellent
vociferous with stats in parliament
about this and that you all debate
who will cleanse this bloody state?

22-11-2007

Collapse of the universe

one day the universe may collapse
a stretch of time will sure demise
any way it is towards disorder
post expansion, it will be wilder
chaos chaos every where
no order any where, dear
can physics predict so precise
to buy the story may I refuse

my children and many a descendant
will still be there fully resplendent
for they the intelligent
can live more fragrant
ye shall sure forever survive
regardless of the time's drive

20-11-2007

Half moon

topless moon, be full soon
oh the shadow makes you moan
sans thee the sky on it's own
sans the moon, my heart not on

18-11-2007

Was that you?

was that you? waiting for none
besides the river, sitting like one
long forgotten, yet alive in
my mind, my memory's inn

timeless thee thy love
ye my drive
till I reach my grave

17-11-2007

Return of a kiss

she said, the kiss "never happened"
for sure I kissed, at her lip's end
I knew not, why now she denies
return my kiss, if not nice
only my lips can take that back
when I said this, she blushed in shock
may be you kissed in my dream
"if so" I said "many a dream"

16-11-2007

The above is the theme of a collection of Arabian poems by Ziad Saudi.

Elite

my dear learned crooked prig
people to you many a pig
now it is clear how you rig
thy malice lo off I shrug

15-11-2007.

That and this

that and this, right or wrong
I concede that you are strong
for fistful of rice, why they throng?
leave them to fate, for how long?

14-11-2007

Warmonger

Oh man, ye not yet grown?
hey! ye no God do not frown
ye shall be, in history so shown
as hunter gatherer ye go down
wars ye wage for what ye clown

13-11-2007

Nobble

you say that is noise
that man's hungry voice
a dying human's nobble
deaf ye Nation noble

12-11-2007

Dear crows

come on my crows to my fields
for you await all the yields
come in groups come as troops
full in black sans the stripes
nefarious notorious be you may
in their shouts in.all they say
once in a year they all pray
thee their father they your prey

11-11-2007

The wisest

Why don't a poem you ink
donkey come take a drink
let us blink blink and blink
till the differences all sink

the wise I saw the riches too
the wisest are only we two

10-11-2007

Lost child

Lost

my child my child
why slipped in wild
the world my child
killed all who willed

Found

my child be bold
mine of you gold
take on who scold
pull down whole world

8-11-2007

Nest

amidst the forest
be my nest
where I rest
rest of my life next

7-11-2007

That is love

remove emotion
remove the passion
rid of despair
rid of the desire
remained a dove?
that is Love!

6-11-2007

Key

I and donkey drank that night
sitting by side he started a fight
told he of my old follies
vowed to swallow all my lilies
drunk I was drunk he was
confused moon looked in haze
mountain winds blew some sounds
still we had few more rounds
drunk I was drunken the donkey
however he has the heaven's key

6-11-2007

Portrait of love

yes or no no more matters
sans desire my heart flutters

I am neither near nor far
with me or not you are

thee timeless thoughtless
ageless joyous lass

you a frozen beam of rays
bring to life memory waves

5-11-2007

Strangers

the more I leave
much more he gave
the more I missed
the more I am blessed
still strangers He and me
one day may end all the alchemy

4-11-2007

Sophistry

hey you thief take your chair
don't know how much I admire
you the richest you the big
what if you had been a pig
make lust with many a boy
you can still act coy and shy
rules are for fools I know you see
smuggler? no they need thy mercy
ye big thief thee I worship
at thy feet all my scholarship

4-11-2007

Being big

To those who are willing
to lose anything
to become big.
listen my friend happiness
is in simplicity and not in being big

O chandamama

Oh brother of my mother
where have you gone hiding
ask vennela please not to bother
why on my heart she likes riding

3-11-2007

Notes:

Chanda = moon. mama = uncle,
Chandamama = an affectionate way of addressing the moon.
It is presumed that vennela [moon light] is the daughter of chandamama.

Entangled

entangled in the twigs
looking as thorny wigs
spilling in sky with red
that tells a tale of blood

oh Sun tired rest
oh Son tried rest
where ever your nest
what ever come next

2-11-2007

Note:

That was a day in Ramadan period. I was also fasting along with my Muslim colleagues [no break fast, no lunch, but I smoked and had tea without sugar and milk where as other colleagues did not smoke and did not take even tea] just voluntarily. Left to myself I do not follow any religion but celebrate all festivals known in India!

Her mind

can I ever ever imagine
waves flowing from her mind
emitting colors that are fine
fragrant that musical sound

look for sparkle in her eye
she may tell by being shy

3-11-2007

Poetlet

let me dear admit
i am not yet a poet
at the worst
if you want
call me a poetlet
some thing like piglet?
or similar to a cutlet!
but call me not a nut
yet if you still insist
i say being nuts is best

1-11-2007

Child

keep mind mild
to live as a child
wondered over a tide
madam ocean's braid
moon rays raid
making her a bride
see the clouds glide
passing by her side
many a drop slide
born lo mermaid

1-11-2007

Dog

dogs bark
unruffled the shark
spark burns bark

31-10-2007

Promise

get me back O god the bygone childhood
let me play promise I will be good
no to naughty I will be just
put me out of this hornet's nest

31-10-2007

Mad

that was a mad moment
only you appeared relevant
every thing else collapsed
in memory that got encased

premises logic failed at that
mad moment yet so resplendent

31-10-2007

Young Varun

My friend young Varun
if you come so sudden
it is all flooded by rain
no rain means no food grain
come dear again and again
but showing some restrain

30-10-2007

Varun= the God of rains!
To my young friend CV Varun
on Sulekha web site, who is just less
than one thirds of my age!!
Age no bar for friendship!!!
Eureka!!!!

Lost

alone when, my thoughts drive
past that lost verve
how full life was so much nerve
lead with love ready to serve

some thing later happened fatal
rise of nettle squeezed mettle

28-10-2007

Thomas Doubting

in every thing you eat
he smells a rat
it is not meant
that you are a cat

he may not spat
even if you want
though you are late
now you are right
he is Thomas Doubt

please laugh not
as it is not
acquired and got
not by default
but by fate

27-10-2007

Night queen

in a cold winter night
when the moon full and bright
sensed that queen of white
ask my heart what a flight

27-10-2007

Queen

That night swept with fragrance afire
the queen quiet in flowing zephyr
filling in the mist soft and loft
the moon mild but some where lost
that light that night my heart that light

O queen quiet set right my heart

27-10-2007

Let us fly

Can not take it any more
come on open thee thy door
no love left in any score
alas the world bitter and sore
as I see scan and scour
let me leave this bloody shore

I shall wait for moon to come
in thy lands to dance and roam
in thy heart my sleep and dream
beside beautiful flowing stream
in to the sky we shall fly
joy or coy with thee I die
come on open thee thy heart
waiting for us the flowery craft

26-10-2007

Gush and glair

gush and glair
went to a fair
to fetch a pail
of fouling oil!
gush got rice
glair not nice
both are mice
shy but twice

25-10-2007

Animal farm

Orwell are you well wakeup man
demons devils dwelling in the farm
meet mr gush a goat but demon
here is glair the other name ram

25-10-2007

Day time moon

moon so dull yesterday came
it was when still the day time
uncared unsung looking pale
to tell perhaps an unfinished tale
not even full moonlight nil
if not night how can it thrill?

An untimely act
loses it's impact

24-10- 07

Escape

blinking blinking dmr
how I wonder what you are
down below the bottle neck
up you came jerking quick

24-10-2007

Soliloquy

dmr dmr
have you any tale
yes sekhar yes sekhar
three books full

24-10-2007

Lap top

Make me your lap top
dance on keys and tap
play music step by step
asleep if, please then stop
boot me not if I forgot
to get you dear sweet or hot
why worry yours my heart!

2007

Only to Indu!

Do not quit

do not
keep quiet
poet or not

say what
you want
poet or not

say just
what
you want
poet or not

say first
what
you want
poet or not

do not
quit
poet or not

quit the quiet
poet or not

Hope

To question is my birth right
may I put as straight as it
I am aware of your might
still I wish to be in fight
I am Hope and glow bright
win or lose I care least
I will fight you you beast
if vampire dies we shall feast

hhov lo the vampire dead
bury it in molten lead
here stops the game of blood
Heaven's blessings to you lad
smiles on faces every one glad
past and forgotten the story sad

22 Oct 07 12:33:10 PM

Hamsafar

As fresh as a forest flower
she came to make me a lover
gave me all that she can shower
can I ever repay? I wonder!!

2007

To Indu with gratitude.

Prayer of a Beggar

God thank you for daily bread
given to me through that maid
first house sixth street city Better
many thanks for not giving butter
I wish my heart sing and flutter
how can it be if it is fatter

please god please don't grant heaven
your children on earth I have seen
living with them for a moment
for your sake I agree though I don't
but in heaven for ever with them?
no God No god don't give scum
better on earth drown in whine
than in heaven with many a swine

2007

A request

I gulp cup after cup
to pulp misery to soup
after that
I blinked at
....
....
my Cup I beg you too
to gulp gulp one or two

2007

Refugee

My thoughts words stopped flowing
my mind now not at all glowing
I flee, as I feel lonely your absence
to escape I wish I lose the sense
refuge I seek in the cup of wine
hei drown see how nice 'n fine

2007

Restless vulture

Innu zarava bhil santal
red indian zulu my pal
beware of her the beautiful
she will beg barrow or steal
to get you enticed full
wants you to be a stone still
in flowing time wearing until
you be dull a void and null

her name is miss Infinity Desire
also some times known as Vampire

world's beauty many a culture
she devoured like a restless vulture
look at the misery of Nagasaki
live and let live, take this Key

2007

Lonely I await

So magical mesmerized that moment
splendid in memory that moment spent
minutes days years decades passed by
yet I remember you playing coy
placed by fate miles and miles apart
in the desert lonely still I await

2007

That night when you came

That night when you came
I was alone in my room
did I say any thing
breeze murmured some thing
did I show you my heart
that was bubbling with joy
we at distances so apart
Vennela, you wanted me to try?

2007

Note: *Vennela in Telugu is Moon light.*

Bubbles

Oh man that simple
hey man why trouble
you man the cannibal
our lives many a bubble
some simple some trouble
simple simple trouble trouble
trouble the simple trouble the bubble
....
what remains? a burst bubble?

2007

Fly's dialogue

Are you busy?
not like a bee!
Oh take it easy!!
it stings you see!!

both flew away
to my dismay

2007

Tell me why

As I don't know I ask
tell me from where
you brought that oil
why that oil smells foul

as I don't know I ask
tell me why
your hands are wet
and why that wet appears red

as I don't know I ask
tell me how many
mothers lost their sons
how many wives became widows

as I don't know I ask
tell me why
those children are weeping
how many are orphans now

tell me why
Oh history Oh mystery
O visionary O missionary

tell me why tell me why
as I don't know I ask
as I don't know I ask

Dead sea

dmr dmr where have you been?
headed to the sea to see how it died
dmr dmr what have you seen?
scene fine relations dead 'n nay lead

2007

Sun, you and me

Call the Sun dark, your sake I may agree
it may be fun for the Sun too, lo that glee
what may not or may we say out of whim
our mutters matter nothing and none to Him

2007

Boundary conditions

Boundaries within boundaries
some by me
some by my men
some by Oman

I cross one
only to find another one

as many I cross
so many yet across

was it wise
to cross the first?

2007

As I don't know

As I don't know I ask
if love exists
when I search to where she exits

As I don't know I ask
if God exists
when I search to where He exits

As I don't know I ask

2007

Oh you

Oh you of those breaking the brain
in search of consciousness grain
can't you see through the body spread
in gene it is, not in the head

2007

Temples of sand

Every time I build a temple
she comes to make it a rubble
who? ask me not the Goddess Herself
lo watch Her playing with the surf

2007

If love exists

If love exists even for a moment
I adore that place that heart
survival depends on environment
for no monument is to be permanent
even if love exists for a moment
I adore it if it survives or not!

2007

Companion

You say you drank poems
I know I drink dreams
when too deep in wine
for sure ye shall shine
for the words remain in brain
Raj you are gentle and fine
Unprovoked companion of mine

2007

Chakravaka

The night is moving
eyes and clouds roving
the moon out of mind
silent the desert sand
relentless across I fly
recklessly high in sky
I will sure reach you
which is since ages due.

2007

Wine

Ye think of me a swine?
as I drink off my wine.
Ok Raj it is all fine I remain.
if not wine what remains mine?
sans wine the world a drain!
wine or none never I whine!!

2007

Sivaranjani

Please come to me
I need you today
in melancholy extreme
my heart resists to sway
we shall again sit at the sea
watch the waves play in spree
I shall set the fret
while it is moonlit

I need you today
heart resists to sway
in the moments of agony
when my eyes are rainy
I think of you and the play
my strings ring smile and sway

2007

To be with her

I stand confused
before her eyes
my heart wavers
worried of her
people are envious
of her beauty and all
I wish
- to be her khol
- her color of henna
- to be with her all the time

As told in Arabic to DMR Sekhar
By Zaid Mazaid, 2007.

The tigress

do not dare to enter that jungle
roams there the Tigress ferocious
she rules alone and stays single
yet commands tough and vivacious

but alas lo the Tigress has a heart
to offer to the prince hale and smart
waits as Saki some times as Maenad
moans in solitude as if crazy or mad

prince charming mr right where to find
restless the Tigress roars to the wind
the forest shivers nothing says the river
Tigress trembles as she looks into mirror

2007

You and me

You me you and none else
finding always new ways
walking along the moon rays
quiet the nights full of grace
flirting with wine that is fine
yet thy presence above Divine

2007

Wise and the foolish alike

Wise and the foolish alike
All those honored men and women
who rose to the heights of heaven
fell not to the ground but still below
there to levels neither high nor low

every body rushing to reach what?
brother to where? ask the smart!
neither he knew nor his Mentor
but running they are, no wonder!

2007

Life

some times mused
some times fused
many times refused
used fused confused?

2007

Sweet Nothings

start smart
mart of art
mart in heart
art of heart
heart in art

what?

revert to start
if naught if knot if not

2007

Ye

Ye smile at me.
Ye say I failed.
I failed? Or
I was failed?
My God!
Thy child failed!!
Thy child failed Thee!!!

2007

New creation

The Sun shook and slipped
the Moon ran away stripped
When I stood up, touching the heaven
Gods demons alike anywhere not to be seen
I shall bring new light, create new Earth
sans tears sans fears sans shears, hence forth.

2007

Kavita

When She comes,
no more I exist
to infinity I exit

Taken to where?
Nothing known, I swear!

Across the woods
around the hills
dwelling through the
dripping beams
cool and calm
whirling swirling
flowing streams.

Conscious or not
woke up or dreamt
I knew not
from where she comes!!

2007

The suspect

You are what you are
I am the suspect
You shall judge
- set me free
- imprison me
- or dissolve me in your dreams
I swear
- by this candle
- by that star, besides the moon
- by the moon light itself
I am yours
Pen your judgment
I will abide

As told in Arabic by Ziad Mazaid to
DMR Sekhar, 2007

Fate of a poem

Like lust loaded inferno
Some made you a porno
They said ye pyramid
Others made ye dirty mud
Playing all games foul
Sans mercy removed thy soul
Then they call you a poem
Alas my poem, my dream
Bereft of green, ye dead tree
Out of senses, they call poetry!

2007

Burma

Iraq in turmoil?
As it has oil!
But why Burma boil?
It's head is a spoil!!

2007

Man in Hell

Oh man, O man, O man,
Oh donkey, O man,O man
Ye camel, O mule, O bull,
Hell in man, man in shell!
Shell in man, man in hell,
Ring the bell, full in hell.

Omen, O man, amen, ameen.
O man, hey man, come on,
Come on, ye man, hey man,
Hey man, ye man, come on,
Bring the bull, blow the shell.
Break the shell, shake the hell.
Bring the bull, ring the bell!
Blow the shell, break the hell!!

2007

A man in stone

Angels listen, his story of the yore,
Found a mermaid, dwelling on the shore.
He frightened the merm, though not intend
Made it up again, while after a mend.
Tender the age, they spoke in signs.
Happy if it shines or in even rains.

Sent he was to a place far 'n different.
Skills he acquired 'n returned confident.
Rushed to the shore, to look at the merm
Now she is young, beauty to the brim

He opened his heart 'n offered it to her
Coy she was, swayed into waves, went too far
Memories in vein, of the days bygone,
Waiting in vain, became he a stone.

2007

Neha, asks, "Tuntul [uncle] what happened to the mermaid?"
Beta, the mermaid married the prince of the ocean, they had children and are very happy.
"then, what about the stone?"
Ages later a goddess saw the stone, turned it into the man there and then she settled

Traitor

Why did you do this and why?
Killed the country? It is now dry!
Ye made a traitor thyself, why?
Sold the old mother? Why and why?
For that pittance of a Nobel prize?
Ye cut the mother to bits and size?
Is not it, is it not a surprise??
Ye still think, these are wise?

Ye say they are well 'n developed!
Methinks...oh they are crooked!!
Ye are proud ye the educated!
But let me be a Spartan Shepard!
Catching fish or tilling Land!!
Ye loot Nature, ye big brigand!!!

2007

Native

I am
- a cloud that can not be rained
- an eye that never swelled
- a river that refused to see the sea
Dry me, try me,,,,
Deny me of my fish and all that I bear

I shall not .....
Mortgage my honour,
maroon my freedom

I am the villager, the native
I shall never desert
My hope
My home
This and more
That is Ziad

Ziad, 2007

As told to DMR Sekhar in Arabic
By the poet Ziad Saudi, a contemporary poet in

On a rainy morning

That rainy morning, I roamed alone
Lazy in village, thinking of none
It is green and serene, seen any where
None to disturb, by buffalo I swear
The butterflies all, were happy and fine
The clouds clasping, still the mountain
The dog, but taking rest
Monkeys busy breaking fast
Smiling slowly, slithering zephyr
Lit my heart with lunar fire
Into the past, the mind's drive
Bringing fast the memories alive
Of childhood plays and dragonflies
College days of daring dreams

At Home

She is my heart!
Is she sweet?
I knew not!!
Sweet or not,
She is great!!!
Keeps me out
of daily fret!
Puts me in many a gust!
She is yes!!...yet...but
Hot, great and very sweet!!!

The road to nowhere

On the road to Nowhere, Ye placed me why?
In wilderness all, even when seen from the sky!
Alone in the unknown, far wider and vast.
From where I knew not, myself I lost!
Where ever I see, it is all the same!!
Whom I came from and who came of me,
no where nearer and none in the realm?
wonder if, it is all an unending dream??

But for the little angel's smile,
presence of Thee so fragile.
They wake me up and make me flow,
Absolutes I cross to see Thy show.
Bless these children for ever and ever,
as they show Thee, here, there and every where!!

Oh my fish

Oh my fish how are you?
None ate thee, what is due?
Timeless are ye, we still view!
Fate in fossil!! What a morgue!!!

2007

A rose in solitude

Moving up high into the sky
from here and there, thick and dry
may be from an oven battery
or it might be a sugar factory
a train or jeep or car or truck
all of them spew that venom black
worse than those napalm bombs
leading us to our own tombs!
Amidst all that chaos and noise
lo that white lovely face
standing in an unknown place
unmindful of human plays
the rose that rose in solitude
pray, she may alter our attitude!!

——— Holy-Fire

based on the verses of Holy-Fire a blogger at Sulekha.com

Setting sun

Look at the setting sun
wearing on yellow crown
wings red, farther spread
moving down westward
here sets, there rises
day 'n night He creates

A girl in prayer

Cadilacross, C adilacross
Ye are sheen lovely a lass
for sure ye, the Grapher's grace
in thee I find eternal peace
silent tunes from ye I hear
is He there to hear you dear?

Behold many a starving mass
without even a blade of grass
pray not for my, daily bread
see the sorrow every where spread
pray for Him the most unblessed
for His kids are severely cursed
Cadilacross, smash the sorrow
in every heart sprout an yarrow.

1979